WORLD SOCCER CLUBS

JUVENTUS

by Derek Moon

Copyright © 2025 by Press Room Editions. All rights reserved. No part of this book may be used or reproduced in any manner whatsoever, including internet usage, without written permission from the copyright owner, except in the case of brief quotations embodied in critical articles and reviews.

Book design by Kate Liestman
Cover design by Kate Liestman

Photographs ©: Giuseppe Maffia/NurPhoto/AP Images, cover; Marco Rosi/Getty Images Sport/Getty Images, 5; Valerio Pennicino/Getty Images Sport/Getty Images, 7, 9, 23; Allsport Hulton/Hulton Archive/Getty Images, 11; Evening Standard/Hulton Archive/Getty Images, 13; Carlo Fumagalli/AP Images, 15; Juventus FC Archive/Getty Images, 17; Mike King/Allsport/Hulton Archive/Getty Images, 19; Claudio Villa/Grazia Neri/Allsport/Getty Images Sport/Getty Images, 21; Zhizhao Wu/Getty Images Sport/Getty Images, 25; Chris Ricco/Getty Images Sport/Getty Images, 27; Claudio Villa/Getty Images Sport/Getty Images, 28

Press Box Books, an imprint of Press Room Editions.

ISBN
978-1-63494-958-3 (library bound)
978-1-63494-972-9 (paperback)
979-8-89469-003-2 (epub)
978-1-63494-986-6 (hosted ebook)

Library of Congress Control Number: 2024912348

Distributed by North Star Editions, Inc.
2297 Waters Drive
Mendota Heights, MN 55120
www.northstareditions.com

Printed in the United States of America
012025

ABOUT THE AUTHOR

Derek Moon is an author who lives in Watertown, Massachusetts, with his wife and daughter.

TABLE OF CONTENTS

CHAPTER 1
STARS OF ITALY 4

CHAPTER 2
THE OLD LADY IS BORN.....10

CHAPTER 3
EUROPEAN POWER.........16

SUPERSTAR PROFILE
ALESSANDRO DEL PIERO....22

CHAPTER 4
UNSTOPPABLE JUVE.......24

QUICK STATS 30
GLOSSARY 31
TO LEARN MORE 32
INDEX..........32

CHAPTER 1

STARS OF ITALY

Juventus fans always expect their team to win. The 2017 Coppa Italia final was no different. The club from Turin, Italy, had won the country's top cup competition two years in a row. Now only Lazio stood in the way of a three-peat.

Lazio came out fast. In the sixth minute, a shot bounced off Juventus's

Paulo Dybala (21) dribbles past a Lazio defender in the 2017 Coppa Italia final.

goal post. That gave Juve a wake-up call. In the 12th minute, Juventus defender Alex Sandro sent a long cross into the penalty area. His teammate Dani Alves volleyed the ball into the net. In the 24th minute, Leonardo Bonucci doubled the lead. The *Bianconeri* (Black and Whites) rolled from there. Juventus secured its third straight Coppa Italia. The job wasn't finished, though.

    The battle for the *scudetto* was tight. Scudetto refers to the championship of Serie A, Italy's top league. Juventus had won the previous five titles. No team had ever won six in a row. Now the club known as the "Old Lady" had a chance to make history.

Mario Mandžukić (left) scored seven Serie A goals during the 2016–17 season.

Four days after the Coppa Italia final, Juve hosted Crotone. A win would secure the scudetto for Juve. The Bianconeri played great defense. They had given up just 26 goals through 36 games that season. But they could also score. Everything came together against Crotone.

Juve goalie Gianluigi Buffon was perfect. Striker Mario Mandžukić scored early. Forward Paulo Dybala doubled the lead before halftime. His bending free kick froze the Crotone goalkeeper. Then Sandro sealed the win with a goal off a corner kick in the 83rd minute.

NEARLY A TREBLE

A treble is when a soccer team wins all three of its biggest competitions in one season. Juventus nearly pulled it off in 2017. First, the team won the Coppa Italia. Then it won Serie A. Only the Champions League remained. That tournament crowns the best club team in Europe. Juventus reached the final. Mario Mandžukić scored on a memorable volley. However, Real Madrid won the match 4–1.

Gianluigi Buffon lifts the Serie A trophy in 2017.

The home crowd roared. The 3–0 win gave Juventus a record sixth straight Serie A championship. Italy's most successful team was at the top once again. And Juventus wasn't showing any signs of slowing down.

9

CHAPTER 2

THE OLD LADY IS BORN

In the late 1800s, soccer spread rapidly around the world. In 1897, the game arrived in Turin. That November, Juventus was founded. The team's name means *youth* in Latin. The name was a nod to the students who formed the club.

The first Juventus teams played in pink jerseys. By 1903, the club needed

John Charles (right) plays in the iconic black-and-white Juventus shirt.

new shirts. Word reached Notts County, a team in England. One of the team's fans shared some black-and-white striped shirts with Juventus. That has been Juve's signature look ever since.

Juventus won its first scudetto in 1904–05. Then, in 1923, the Agnelli family bought Juventus. The Agnellis owned Fiat,

BITTER RIVALS

In 1906, some fans soured on Juventus. The club didn't represent their working-class roots. So, those fans joined forces with another team to create Torino FC. Juventus and Torino remain fierce rivals. Juventus also has rivals from other cities. Games between Juve and Inter Milan are especially heated. They are nicknamed the *Derby d'Italia*.

Giampiero Boniperti (left) and John Charles (right) inspect the field ahead of a game in 1958.

Italy's biggest car company. Their wealth helped turn Juventus into a powerhouse.

In 1926, the team won its second league title. Then it won five in a row starting in 1931. Gianpiero Combi led those teams. Many considered him the best goalkeeper in the world.

Around this time, a reporter was impressed after watching Juventus defeat Genoa. He called Juve the "Old Lady" in his match report. No one knows for sure why he used that name. It may have been because of the club's history and tradition. Whatever the reason, the nickname stuck.

Juventus took a step backward in the years surrounding World War II (1939–1945). Then Giampiero Boniperti arrived as a teenager in 1947. His 21 goals helped Juve win the league title in 1950. Juve won another in 1952. Soon, John Charles and Omar Sívori joined Boniperti on the forward line. Behind the *Trio Magico* (Magic Trio), Juve won Serie A in 1958, 1960, and 1961.

Omar Sívori (left) scored 165 goals for Juventus.

Juventus dominated in Italy. The team won its 13th scudetto in 1967. No club had won more. The club had fans across the country. And yet the Bianconeri were about to get even better.

CHAPTER 3

EUROPEAN POWER

Juventus didn't want Dino Zoff at first. The team told the teenage goalie he was too small. The club changed its mind in 1972. The 30-year-old Zoff arrived at Juve as a calm veteran. Over his 11 seasons with the club, Juve won six more league titles. The team also reached its first European Cup final in 1973.

Dino Zoff (center) recorded 227 shutouts for Juventus.

That tournament is now called the Champions League.

While Zoff locked down the defense, forward Roberto Bettega piled up goals. In 1976, Giovanni Trapattoni took over as manager. He coached his talented squads to play as one unit. Their disciplined structure shut down opponents. In 1982, Trapattoni led Juve to its 20th scudetto.

That summer, Michel Platini arrived. The French midfielder could create scoring chances like few others. His accurate passes found just the right spots. Yet he could also score. Behind Platini, Juve reached the 1983 European Cup final. The Bianconeri made it back to the final two years later. And this time, they won.

Michel Platini recorded 104 goals and 49 assists for Juventus during his career.

Platini scored the game's only goal against Liverpool. That secured Juve's first European title.

In the early 1990s, Juventus rebuilt around Alessandro Del Piero. The forward could rip a powerful shot with his right or left foot. That helped him rack up goals. Del Piero propelled Juve to the 1996 Champions League final. The Old Lady's opponent, Ajax, was looking for its second straight title. The game went to extra time tied 1–1. Juve then won in a shootout.

The next season, Juventus added Zinedine Zidane to its stacked squad. The French midfielder possessed great vision and playmaking skills. Over five seasons, he became one of the world's best players. Zidane led Juve to the 1997 and 1998 Champions League finals.

HEYSEL STADIUM DISASTER

Tragedy overshadowed Juventus's win in the 1985 European Cup. Hooligan culture was at its peak. Prior to the game, Liverpool fans charged Juventus supporters. A wall collapsed during the chaos. Eventually, 39 people died. Hundreds more were injured.

Many soccer fans consider Zinedine Zidane (21) to be one of the greatest midfielders of all time.

Zidane left Juventus in 2001. The team didn't struggle without him, though. It quickly reloaded around Pavel Nedvěd. Behind the creative midfielder, Juve won Serie A titles in 2002 and 2003. The team also reached another Champions League final in 2003. Opponents could only envy Juve's star power and success.

SUPERSTAR PROFILE

ALESSANDRO DEL PIERO

Many big stars have come and gone from Juventus. Alessandro Del Piero stayed with the club as long as he could. The Italian forward arrived at Juve as a teenager in 1993. He finally left in 2012. But he wanted to stay longer. He even said he'd play for free. The team had other ideas, though.

A natural scorer, Del Piero always seemed to come through for his team. No Juventus player can match his 289 goals. He also led the team to great heights. Juventus won Serie A six times with Del Piero. He helped Juve win the 1996 Champions League. But for many fans, Del Piero's loyalty was what set him apart. He stuck with the team through good times and bad. No one has played more than his 705 matches with the Old Lady.

Alessandro Del Piero scored a career-high 21 Serie A goals in both 1997–98 and 2007–08.

CHAPTER 4

UNSTOPPABLE JUVE

Juventus won Serie A again in 2005. It marked the team's sixth scudetto in 11 seasons. However, the club got caught in a cheating scandal. As a punishment, Juventus had to forfeit the 2005 and 2006 scudettos. The team was also sent to Italy's second division for the 2006–07 season.

No one has played in more Serie A games than Gianluigi Buffon, who appeared in 657.

Many of Juve's biggest stars left. But goalie Gianluigi Buffon and forward Alessandro Del Piero stayed. So did Giorgio Chiellini, Pavel Nedvěd, and David Trezeguet. Those players led Juventus to first place in Serie B. As a result, the team earned its way back to Serie A. Fans always adored those players for staying.

In 2011–12, former Juve star Antonio Conte returned as manager. His team

SUPPORTERS EVERYWHERE

Juventus is Italy's most popular club. Turin is in the northern part of the country. But the team is especially popular in southern Italy. In the mid-1900s, many people moved north to work at the Fiat plant. While there, they became fans of Juventus.

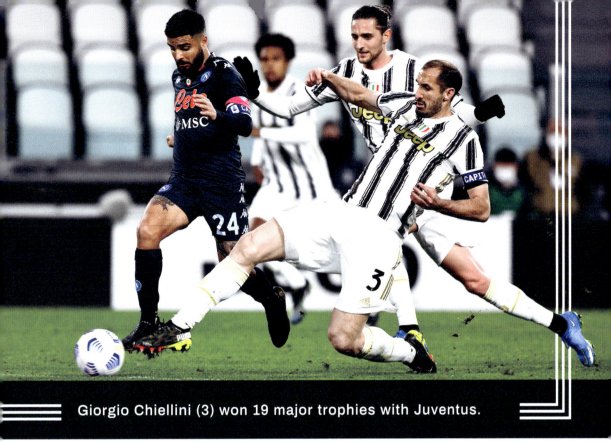
Giorgio Chiellini (3) won 19 major trophies with Juventus.

didn't lose a league game all season. That began a period of historic success. From 2012 to 2020, Juventus won nine straight Serie A titles. Some of them weren't even close. Before 2012, no Juve team had won more than 28 games in Serie A. The team surpassed that four times during this run. The 2013–14 team won 33 games.

27

Andrea Pirlo recorded 13 Serie A assists in 2011–12, his first season with Juventus.

Juventus has a long tradition of superstar players. That continued during the 2010s. Buffon and Chiellini anchored the back line. They were joined by Leonardo Bonucci in 2010. Veteran midfielder Andrea Pirlo arrived in 2011. Midfield prodigy Paul Pogba followed a year later. Those players led Juve to the 2015 Champions League final. Pirlo and Pogba soon left. Still, Juve reached the Champions League final again in 2017. However, Juventus lost both times.

Juventus had finished as Europe's runner-up a record seven times. The team spent big to try to change that. In 2018, it brought in superstar forward Cristiano Ronaldo. He scored a ton of goals in his three seasons. His scoring didn't always result in wins, though. Juve's run of league titles ended in 2021. Ronaldo left soon after. The team was still chasing its third European title. But with Juve's long tradition of success, fans knew that could change at any time.

QUICK STATS

JUVENTUS

Founded: 1897

Home stadium: Allianz Stadium

Serie A titles: 36

European Cup/Champions League titles: 2

Coppa Italia titles: 15

Key managers:

- Giovanni Trapattoni (1976–86, 1991–94): 6 Serie A titles, 2 Coppa Italia titles

- Marcello Lippi (1994–99, 2001–04): 5 Serie A titles, 1 Champions League title, 1 Coppa Italia title

- Massimiliano Allegri (2014–19, 2021–24): 5 Serie A titles, 5 Coppa Italia titles

Most career appearances: Alessandro Del Piero (705)

Most career goals: Alessandro Del Piero (289)

Stats are accurate through the 2023–24 season.

GLOSSARY

forfeit
To lose something as a penalty.

free kick
A play where a team gets to kick a dead ball after a foul by the opposing team.

hooligan
A young troublemaker, often associated with a soccer team.

penalty area
The 18-yard box in front of the goal where a player is granted a penalty kick if he or she is fouled.

prodigy
A young person with exceptional skill.

rivals
Opposing players or teams that bring out the greatest emotion from fans and players.

scandal
An event that many people find shocking or disgraceful.

shootout
A way of deciding a tie game. Players from each team take a series of penalty kicks.

veteran
A player who has spent several years in a league.

volleyed
Kicked the ball while it was still in the air.

TO LEARN MORE

Hewson, Anthony K. *GOATs of Soccer*. North Mankato, MN: Abdo Publishing, 2022.

Marthaler, Jon. *The Best Teams of World Soccer*. Minneapolis: Abdo Publishing, 2024.

Snow, Kevin. *Juventus FC*. New York: Cavendish Square, 2021.

MORE INFORMATION

To learn more about Juventus go to **pressboxbooks.com/AllAccess**. These links are routinely monitored and updated to provide the most current information available.

INDEX

Alves, Dani, 6

Bettega, Roberto, 18
Boniperti, Giampiero, 14
Bonucci, Leonardo, 6, 28
Buffon, Gianluigi, 8, 26, 28

Charles, John, 14
Chiellini, Giorgio, 26, 28
Combi, Gianpiero, 13
Conte, Antonio, 26

Del Piero, Alessandro, 19, 22, 26
Dybala, Paulo, 8

Mandžukić, Mario, 8

Nedvěd, Pavel, 21, 26

Pirlo, Andrea, 28–29
Platini, Michel, 18–19
Pogba, Paul, 28–29

Ronaldo, Cristiano, 29

Sandro, Alex, 6, 8
Sívori, Omar, 14

Trapattoni, Giovanni, 18
Trezeguet, David, 26

Zidane, Zinedine, 20–21
Zoff, Dino, 16, 18